Facts About the Rockhopper Penguin

By Lisa Strattin

© 2016 Lisa Strattin

Revised © 2019

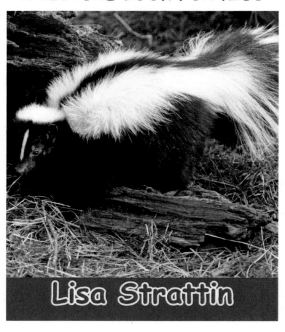

FACTS ABOUT THE
SKUNK
A PICTURE BOOK FOR KIDS

Lisa Strattin

Facts for Kids Picture Books by Lisa Strattin

Sign Up for New Release Emails Here

http://LisaStrattin.com/subscribe-here

All information in this book has been carefully researched and checked for factual accuracy. However, the author and publisher makes no warranty, express or implied, that the information contained herein is appropriate for every individual, situation or purpose and assume no responsibility for errors or omissions. The reader assumes the risk and full responsibility for all actions, and the author will not be held responsible for any loss or damage, whether consequential, incidental, special or otherwise, that may result from the information presented in this book.

All images are free for use or purchased from stock photo sites or royalty free for commercial use.

Some coloring pages might be of the general species due to lack of available images.

I have relied on my own observations as well as many different sources for this book and I have done my best to check facts and give credit where it is due. In the event that any material is used without proper permission, please contact me so that the oversight can be corrected.

Contents

INTRODUCTION

Penguins are birds that live in very cold places. They do not fly in the air. In fact, penguins have flippers because to swim underwater. There are 17 different species of penguins! The Rockhopper Penguin is one of these. You can find these birds in a place close to Antarctica called the Falkland Islands. They are also found on islands south of New Zealand which is a country on the opposite side of the world and far south of the Equator.

Rockhopper Penguins are among the smallest of the penguins. Two features make them look different: 1) dark red eyes and 2) a crest of long and thin black and yellow feathers on the top of its head.

They are very good swimmers and fast too! They can swim up to 20 miles per hour. That's much faster than you can swim. They also can hold their breath under the water for as long as 20 minutes.

CHARACTERISTICS

These are very social birds that live together in large groups called colonies. When they are done swimming in the ocean, they land on a rock at the edge of the water and then hop up using both feet together to jump from that rock to the next rock. This hopping behavior is how they got their name.

They make loud sounds when calling out to their mates or chicks or while defending their nests.

APPEARANCE

The chicks look like little grey fluff balls with feet and a beak! But once they mature into adults, they have the typical white front and black coat of other penguins. They develop dark red eyes and a crest of black and yellow feathers that stick out the top and sides of the head. The feathers on the rest of their bodies lie thick and flat against their skin to help keep them warm against the cold weather.

Instead of wings, these birds have flippers, one on each side, plus a short tail. They have two pink colored webbed feet with rounded nails at the end of their toes for gripping onto slippery wet rocks.

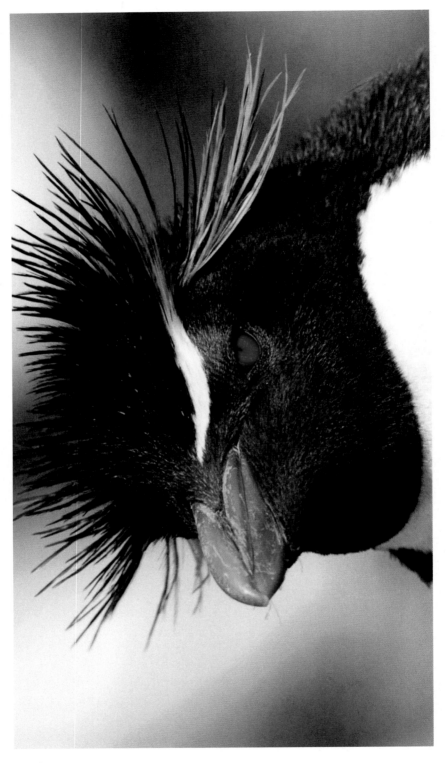

LIFE STAGES

This bird starts out as an egg from the mother. Both parents will take turns keeping the egg warm while it incubates. In just over a month, a new chick will break out of its egg. The chick is totally dependent on its parents for warmth, protection, and food.

Between two and three months later, the chick will lose its soft baby down and grow adult feathers. Now they are called juveniles, kind of like teenagers. But they are capable of swimming and catching food on their own. Soon they are adults, this is the last and longest stage of life.

LIFE SPAN

The average life span of these penguins is about 10 years in the wild, and some have been known to live up to 20 years.

SIZE

These penguins measure from 16 to 20 inches tall. The males are bigger than the females.

HABITAT

Rockhopper Penguins live in the cold regions of the Southern Hemisphere. They do migrate two times per year due to the change of season and weather conditions. This means that the whole group moves together from one place to another place that is far away and then, six months later, the group travels back to the first place.

They prefer to live on the rocks and cliffs that are next to the ocean. This way they have some protection from predators when they are out of the water. They always stay close to the ocean, which is important because that is where they hunt for their food.

DIET

Rockhoppers are carnivores, that means they eat meat. Their favorite food is krill which are very tiny shrimp-like marine creatures. They also eat small cold-water fish such as anchovies and smelt. Sometimes they will also eat small squids or octopus.

FRIENDS AND ENEMIES

Some sea birds, like the albatross, pose no threat to penguins, so these two different types of birds will often nest near each other and be friendly.

All penguins avoid orcas (killer whales) and seals because those animals will kill and eat them. Another enemy is the Skua, a large sea gull-like seabird, that may carry off a baby chick for dinner.

Believe it or not, humans can also be enemies, indirectly. This happens when commercial fisherman "overfish." They take too many fish out of the seas all at once. As a result, the penguins have less food to catch and eat, and some of them do not survive.

SUITABILITY AS PETS

The rockhopper penguins are cute-looking birds with a comical waddle-walk that make people laugh and smile. They seem friendly, especially when you see them in a zoo taking a fish right from the hand of a trainer. But the truth is they are not suitable to be a pet in your home. They are still wild animals.

You cannot keep them in a cage or in your bathtub. They cannot be taught to use a litter box or walk on a leash. It would be very cruel to take one away from its colony, which is its family. Even if you tried to take good care of it, most likely it would get sick due to stress and die.

It is a much better idea to enjoy penguins by watching them on a nature documentary or perhaps at the zoo. They should be left alone to live a full and natural life.

COLOR ME

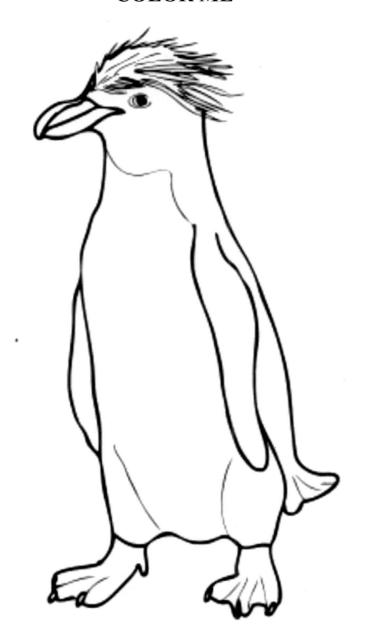

COLOR ME

COLOR ME

COLOR ME

COLOR ME

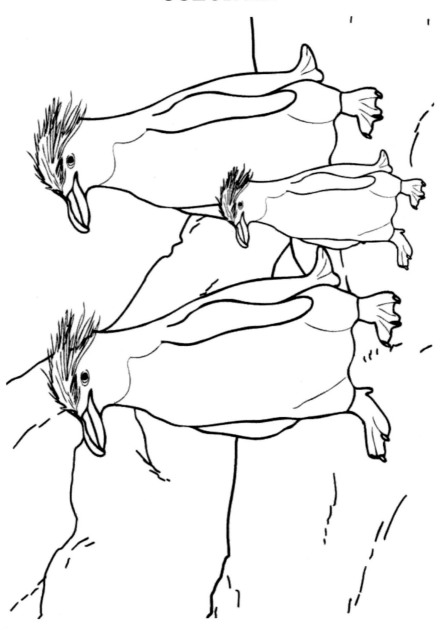

COLOR ME

COLOR ME

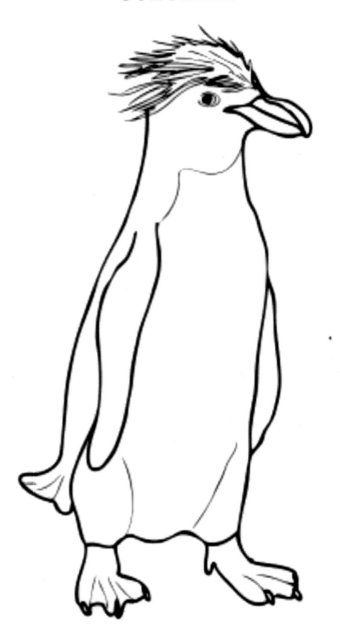

COLOR ME

COLOR ME

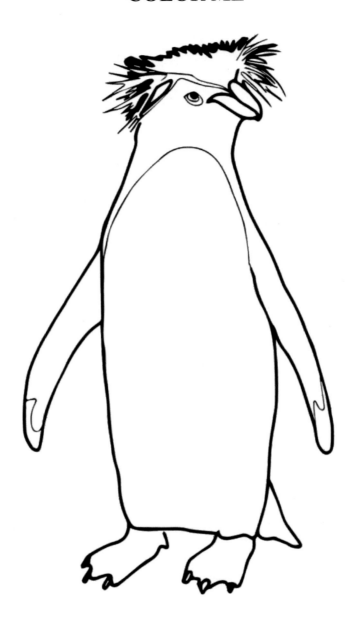

Please leave me a review here:

http://lisastrattin.com/Review-Vol-163

For more Kindle Downloads Visit Lisa Strattin
Author Page **on Amazon Author Central**

http://amazon.com/author/lisastrattin

To see upcoming titles, visit my website at
LisaStrattin.com– **all books available on kindle!**

http://lisastrattin.com

FREE BOOK

FOR ALL SUBSCRIBERS

LisaStrattin.com/Subscribe-Here

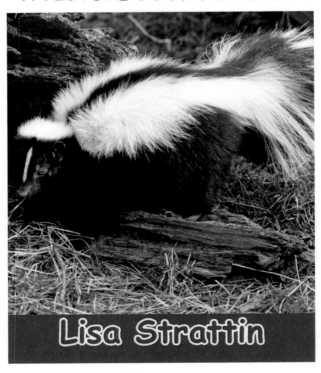

FACTS ABOUT THE
SKUNK

A PICTURE BOOK FOR KIDS

Lisa Strattin

24380729R00026